Victorian and Edwardian

HORSES

from Historic Photographs

Victorian and Edwardian

HORSES

from Historic Photographs

Introduction and commentaries by
DAVID H. KENNETT

B.T. BATSFORD LTD
LONDON

By the same author

Anglo-Saxon Pottery
Portrait of Bedfordshire
Norfolk Villages
Guide to County History – Bedfordshire

Frontispiece: see page 96
Opposite: see page 91

First published 1980
Reprinted 1984
Text copyright © David H. Kennett
Filmset in Monophoto Apollo by
Servis Filmsetting Limited, Manchester
Printed by
Butler & Tanner Ltd, Frome, Somerset
for the Publishers, B.T. Batsford Limited
4 Fitzhardinge Street, London W1H 0AH
ISBN 0 7134 1569 X

CONTENTS

ACKNOWLEDGMENTS

I have incurred many debts in the making of this book. To all the librarians, museum officers and private individuals who have aided my search for Victorian and Edwardian horses from old photographs, I tender my most heartfelt thanks. I am particularly grateful to two institutions: Norwich City Library and Luton Museum. At the latter, I have been almost a permanent fixture of the students' room for many years. Its superb collections of social history materials have proved of great value both in this study and in more general terms. For the guidance and good humour of Marion Nicholls and Clare Fleck I am more than grateful. I am indebted to my publishers, B.T. Batsford, and particularly to Samuel Carr for considerable assistance and for providing another collection of photographs, complementary in origin to that which my efforts had assembled. My final debt is that which all authors make; it is none the less real. Only I know that without Susan's aid and companionship, this volume would have been more delayed than it was in its completion.

Photographs 45 and 109 appear by gracious permission of Her Majesty The Queen. The author and the publishers would also like to thank the following for permission to include their photographs in this book: Atherton Public Library, 23; Birmingham Reference Library, 13, 86; Croydon Public Library, 114; E. Dennis, Scarborough, 34; Derby Museums and Art Gallery, 110, 111, 112, 115; Eastgate House Museum, Rochester, 75; A.R. Edney, Oxfordshire, 72; English China Clays Ltd, 103, 104, 105; Flintshire Record Office, 38; R.A. Gardner, Eynsham, Oxfordshire, 65; F.J. Garrett and M. Haird, 22; Great Yarmouth Public Library, 56, 92; Henley-in-Arden Guildhall, 30; Highgate Library, 80; Mrs Hylton-Foster, 48; Mrs Hazel James, Bodmin, 31; The Jockey Club, Newmarket, 53, 54, 55; Leicestershire Museums, Art Galleries and Record Office, 32, 49, 50, 51, 66, 67, 70, 113, 116; Linenhall Library, Belfast, 61; London Transport Board, 85; Lord Londonderry, 43; Luton Museum and Art Gallery, 46, 59, 62, 100; Museum of East Anglian Life, Stowmarket, 4, 16; Museum of English Rural Life, Reading, 18, 24, 35; National Army Museum, 107, 108, 120; National Library of Wales, 64; National Library of Ireland, 44; National Museum of Wales, 93; Norwich City Library, 19, 26, 28, 29, 41, 57, 58, 71, 73, 87, 99, 101, 119; K. Oates, 20; Salford Public Library, 90; SKF (UK) Ltd, Luton, 102; Stranraer Public Library, 7; Suffolk Photographic Survey, Ipswich, 5, 8, 9, 11; Ulster Folk Museum, 10; D.C. Vosper Collection, 37; Warwickshire Record Office, 76; Wisbech and Fenland Museum, Wisbech, 21. Photograph 60 is from the author's own collection.

THE PHOTOGRAPHERS

Not all of the photographers are known, but the following are certainly represented in the collection chosen:

Patrick Baron, 76
A.P. Cooper, Norwich, 58
W.H. Cox, Luton, 100
P.H. Emerson, Norfolk, 87
F.E. Gibson, Penzance and
   Scilly Isles, 6 and 91
W.A. Green, Ulster, 10
T.G. Hobbs, Luton, 69, 74, 98

J. Hughes, Flintshire, 38
A.J. Lessir, Birmingham, 13
F.J. Smith, Cambridgeshire, 22
Symmons and Thiele, London, 117
Fox Talbot, Lacock, Wiltshire, 42
Stanley Thurston, Luton, 46
York and Son, Notting Hill,
   London, 78, 79, 82

INTRODUCTION

3   Exmoor ponies awaiting sale

The Horse, ubiquitous in Victorian England, was rather less prevalent in the Edwardian era. In the latter period new forms of transport were important: the motor car, the electric tram, the trolleybus, the motor omnibus. Only on the farm did the horse retain its primacy until after the Great War. Queen Victoria's death, on 22 January 1901, neatly closes the age of the horse. In August of the same year, the *Daily Mail* noted of the movements of her son, King Edward VII,

> the king reached Marlborough House, having travelled up from Windsor in his motor car.

Saddlery and Harness, the monthly trade journal, was rightly alarmed. It quoted the sentence and continued,

> These are words of great moment to the harness trade, which will, probably, cause many a harness maker to "scratch his head where it doesn't itch".

The advent of the motor car in the royal household certainly caused redundancies in the royal stables at Windsor and in London.

The change is similar to that which happened in the less-elevated world of commerce. In 1903 there were 3,623 horse-buses in London and only thirteen motor-buses; ten years later of the 3,664 buses in London, only 142 were horse-buses. The hansom cab (81) too became a declining sight on the streets of London in the Edwardian years: the 11,000 in 1903 shrank to a mere 1,900 in 1913. These were dramatic changes not confined to the capital. In Leicester, the horse trams (66) ceased to operate on 18 May 1904. In the same city, the first motor parcel van was in use in December 1910, while two other indicators of change are equally precise. The Birmingham horse market ceased to occupy its traditional site on 22 July 1901 and the carriage trade's advertisements show a distinct shift in emphasis. In *Kelly's Directory for Hertfordshire*, the Hertford carriage makers, H. McMullen & Son, had 13 horse-drawn vehicles on their page in the

1896 edition. The variety was considerable: double victoria, stanhope waggonette, sporting phaeton, Manchester cart, hooded stanhope, governess cart and victoria were those named; the brougham and others were not designated. In the 1910 edition of the same directory, the same firm took a half-page advertisement. It described them as 'Motor Body and Carriage Builders'; the vehicle was an early motor car.

It was in personalised and urban transport that the change away from the horse was most rapid in Edwardian England. Elsewhere horses were replaced more gradually. In agriculture, the number of horses used on farms reached a peak of something over a million in 1891 and remained at this number steadily to the Great War. The process is best seen in a microcosm. In Bedfordshire, a rural county, farm horses whose numbers had been steady since 1884 rose between 1902 and 1905 from 12, 310 to 13,090. Their numbers had marginally risen by 1909, but in 1913 the decline had just begun. The Great War, however, seems to have halted the decline in farm horses in this county as the figures, at just above 11,000, are static from 1913 to 1923. Yet even here there was a 15% loss in the number of horses from the earlier peak. A similar loss can be seen in the decline of farm horses in Norfolk between 1903 and 1924, respectively computed at 46,849 and 39,107. The more rapid adoption of tractors in the inter-war years is reflected in the halving of the number of horses in use on Bedfordshire's farms by 1938, even though the market gardening area of the eastern part of the county found a single-horse plough more economical than a tractor-driven one and the animal could also be used to pull the produce cart to market or the station. Tractors in fact remained less in numbers than horses until 1950; a decade earlier the 650,000 horses used on British farms exerted a greater pulling power than the tractive capacity of all tractors when expressed in terms of their horse-power.

'Horse-power': the word was natural to Victorian engineers when they sought a measure of the capacity of their steam and other engines. The practice continued. Motor cars were marketed in terms of their horse-power until well after the Second World War. The great *Mallard* locomotive on 3 July 1938 achieved the speed of 126mph with a tractive capacity of 26 drawbar horsepower. The much earlier comparison reflected the ubiquity of the horse in Victorian England.

Victorian England, indeed, was the great age of the horse. The numbers increased steadily from 1837 to 1901, partly with the increasing wealth of the country, partly because to possess a horse was to be seen to have arrived, in the social sense, at least. A Victorian ladies' journal, *Leisure Hour*, in its issue of June 1892, commented that there were

> 300,000 horses in London, not a tenth of what there are in this island, but what a herd it seems. Taking them at £25 a piece, they would run up to £7.5 million and that would be putting them at a low price. To keep them at less than half a sovereign a week we should require seven and a half million [pounds] a year and if we add to this, the current cost, the interest on the capital sunk in them and their harness, the wages paid in looking after them and the rent of their stables we shall get to high figures that look almost too large to be true.

Yet surprisingly to contemporaries, it was true. The estimate and the quotation repeated in *Saddlery and Harness* can be backed by the cold statistics of agricultural returns and taxation figures for vehicles and trade horses. Only gentlemen's horses were exempt. Of these an estimate of half a million was made in 1888; they formed a comparatively minor element in the horse population of Britain and Ireland.

More significant were trade horses; they were an element of every conceivable industry. Hansom cabs each required two horses to keep going; the vehicle was more productive than the animal pulling it. Huge fleets of horses were kept by all the railway companies with stables to match. Here they had many uses. Directly in shunting, a use to which private companies with sidings also put horses (99), the railway companies also used horses for activities ancillary to their business. The largest ownership of horses in Victorian England was by the railway companies, particularly in their freight divisions. Their use was to take goods to the customer's doors. Even in a small town like Luton, Bedfordshire, (population, 5,000 in 1851 and 36,000 in 1901), the Great Northern Railway had to build a stable block capable of holding a hundred or more horses as late as 1908. For the hat trade alone they had 18 drays in 1904; the rival, the Midland Railway, had an even larger fleet (100). Similar observations could be made about the railway horses of other towns: hosiery in Leicester, stockings in Nottingham, steel and cutlery in Sheffield. Even a new technology of the twentieth century, ball bearings, needed horse-drawn drays to transport the finished products away from the factory (102).

The horse bus was universal in late Victorian towns. There could be a single horse or as many as three (63), but two was the most usual number of horses (64, 65, 84). The later horse-tram could have a single horse (66) or two (85). Each vehicle required an average of eleven horses to keep it on the road; a turn of the century figure for the number of bus-horses is in the order of a quarter of a million; the peak figure was perhaps half as much again.

Probably as many horses were used by the drink trade; both breweries and mineral water manufacturers kept horses for their carts, drays and waggons (92–98). Deliveries too were made by horse-and-cart, a panier cart for meat (74) or a more sturdy vehicle for heavier goods like coal. In Ireland and remoter parts of Scotland, horseback was used (33); a peat cart, too, required a horse (88).

The ubiquity of the horse meant that it was more often than not incidental to a photograph rather than the central subject. Photography of horses in Victorian Brtain had two strands: the deliberate and the casual. The latter was more frequent; under half the photographs selected for this book seem to have been deliberately taken to show the horse. Almost any street scene in any town taken between 1851 and 1901 would have been incomplete without a horse or a horse-drawn vehicle; many later ones similarly have vehicles in them drawn by the horse. Only London and other large cities experienced saturation: there was a Royal Commission on London Traffic in 1906 and this was a perhaps belated response to the growing congestion. London Bridge (78) and other vantage points in the City and the West End (79, 80) were the most crowded places. But the horse was everywhere. The carrier's cart was a commonplace of market day in most towns from the largest to the most minuscule, and men in villages made a living from being the carrier (27), although as with some horse-trades it may have been combined with keeping the village inn, or less commonly with being the miller or the baker. The travelling shop from Cambridgeshire (22) is not unique.

The deliberate photography of horses begins in the first decade of the art form. Our selection includes one by the celebrated pioneer of photography, Henry Fox Talbot, taken as early as 1843 (42). The gentleman's carriage outside his house remained a favourite theme: another example dates to c.1912 (40). The family in its vehicle is the theme of a number of the photographs (23, 26) and allied to this, the outing takes its place among the photographs made as an act of record (37, 61). Some people may have wished to have been photographed driving their carriage (46, 47). In the case of Madame de Falbe (46) it was a commissioned photograph; she was an accomplished horsewoman.

Some other photographs with horses were also acts of record. The mayoral or sheriff's carriage (75, 76) is one obvious example, although King Edward VII in Dublin (77) may be considered an item of news. Most parades of which photographs have survived similarly belong to this category of record photographs. The parades could be military (114, 115, 117), of the circus through a town prior to the performances (59), of the May Queen (60), or even of the Sunday school treat (58). The lavish funeral procession (69) is another example.

Distinctly taken because of the excellence of the horse or of the horse and vehicle are those photographs of the successful horse. Racehorses (53, 54) are an obvious example, although here it should be noted that more often the record was a painting until well after the Great War. Some horses won for their owners and drivers trophies in competitions (94, 97) and this clearly inspired the surviving photograph.

Another defined group of horse-photographs are those either where the horse is on duty for the first time, a rare event in Victorian and Edwardian times, or for the last time. The final journey of the horse-drawn mail cart (91) is a subject commemorated, but as far as is known none of the photographs in this book are of *the last* day of a bus or tram service. They all seem to have been taken while horses were the main motive power for town vehicles (63–66, 84, 85). Similarly the last use of horses on a farm is not commemorated in this book; examples of such photographs do exist, but their date is well into the 1930s. One photograph (9) seems indeed to be of the acquisition of a new machine, but the tractive power was still the horse.

Also recording a 'first' is the photograph of Lord Charles Cavendish Bentinck (111); it was his first parade and the family felt justifiably proud of him. Personal record probably lies behind some of the photographs taken in the Crimean War (107–109) although at least one (109) was later commercially reproduced. Not all Crimean War photographs, however, are simply those of record; those taken by Fenton were very much War Office propaganda to counter-act charges of inefficiency at the front, but as far as is known none of these is reproduced herein. Personal record would account too for Lady Maureen Stewart on her pony (43) and probably for Madame de Falbe in her phaeton (46).

Most owners of horses had a pride in their animal: the boy with his shire horse, most obviously (4), but probably also the two Suffolk punches (8). A similar pride in their turnout doubtless lies behind the photographs of fire brigades (68, 101).

The final category of horse photographs which can be delineated are those taken for advertising or other propaganda. In Luton the two railway companies waged an unceasing battle for the very considerable carrying trade generated by the hat industry. The drays with hat crates (100) is part of the Midland Railway's propaganda against its rival, the Great Northern Railway. Both companies' vehicles figure in the work of another Luton photographer, T.G. Hobbs, who in 1908 persuaded the businessmen of the growing town to finance a lavish booklet, *Luton and its Neighbourhood Illustrated*, designed to help attract new industry to the town (69, 74, 98). The genre is common for most thriving and expanding towns in the 1890s and the Edwardian era. A similar production for London, *The Queen's London*, has also been used in the selection of our photographs (78, 79, 82, 117). These productions have assumed considerable value as contemporary records of great cities and small towns.

Small town, great city, isolated farm or mere village, their inhabitants could not do without the horse in Victorian England and only in the great city was some replacement made in the Edwardian years. Our photographs are intended to reflect what has been called the horse-drawn society.

This introduction has derived much profit from two pieces on horses and society both by Professor F.M.L. Thompson, his inaugural lecture, *Victorian England: the horse-drawn society* (Bedford College, University of London, 1970), and a paper entitled 'Nineteenth-Century Horse Sense' in *Economic History Review*, volume 29 no. 1, February 1976, pages 60–81. The latter provides greater statistics than have been quoted here.

4   The boy took great pride in the grooming of his shire horse, seen here with full harness on an unknown Norfolk farm about 1900

THE FARM

5 Two horses were necessary to pull the single-handed Suffolk wooden plough still used in the Stowmarket district in Edwardian times. The third horse is spare and could be coupled if the going became too arduous

6 A single-horse metal plough being used prior to planting the bulbs at St Martin's, Isles of Scilly; the plough is being guided by a boy and the horse led by a woman

7 A single horse between shafts pulling a disc scuffer. The implement is said to have been invented by John McNeillie, Garlieston Smithy, in Galloway

8 Harrowing at Coddenham, Suffolk,
with a multi-tined harrow drawn by
two Suffolk punches. The equipment
was used well beyond the time of the
Great War

9 While the machinery of Edwardian agriculture was more mechanised than its Victorian predecessors the tractive power was still supplied by horses. This reaper and binder was at work at Mendlesham, Suffolk, in 1905. It required two horses to pull it

10 Reaping corn with a two-horse rick engine at Toombridge, County Antrim, about 1917

11 *Below left* A sail-reaper at Happisburgh, Norfolk, drawn by two horses. The sailer has a platform onto which the corn falls as it is cut and the man guided the horses by reins from his seat on the outside of the sailer. Photograph of about 1910

12 *Below* A single-horse rake standing in a reaped field near Beverley, Yorkshire

13 Haymaking on 16 July 1890 on a farm near Birmingham. The photograph was taken at 2.30pm

14 Four horses in tandem pulling a
loaded waggon. They were Sir
Cuthbert Quiller's punches

15 Mechanised haymaking at Burton Barber, Leicestershire, during the Edwardian years. The waggon is ready to cart away bags of corn which have been threshed in the steam-threshing machine in the background

16 Up to the Great War, horses
were fully occupied during the
harvest. At George Last's farm,
Cranley Green, Eye, Suffolk, in 1914,
one horse pulls a Suffolk waggon
loaded with hay while another rests
grazing off hay being made into a
rick. Ideally five horses were used for
three waggons

17 Carting wood on a Sussex waggon; three horses are used in tandem

18 *Left* Carting faggots on a spindle-sided bow waggon, with two horses paired. The waggon is of a type in use in the Cotswolds and the Chilterns around 1900

19 *Below* At the end of the day; the boy guides two shire horses past Acle blacksmith's shop pulling their plough raised on blocks. This Norfolk scene dates to around the turn of the century

20 A horse charabanc arriving at Histon, Cambridgeshire, with fruit pickers, about 1910. The pickers had come to harvest strawberries

THE COUNTRYSIDE

21 Carters and carriers outside The Swan with Two Necks at Swavesey, Cambridgeshire, c.1890. The bags probably contained both agricultural produce and coal

22 The villages of late Victorian and Edwardian England were often supplied by a travelling stock of household goods. Mr C. Brown of Gwydir Street, Cambridge, took his two-horse dray round the neighbouring villages. He is shown at Cottenham, c.1910

23 A family out for a drive in their Manchester cart at Gib Fold Farm, near Atherton, Lancashire, about 1910. Note the holders for parasols and umbrellas and the side lights

24 Two men out for a Sunday
evening drink in summer in Somerset,
1912. The wheels of the trap have 16
spokes, an unusually large number

25 The pony and trap of W. Ambler of Dewsbury outside The Three Nuns Inn, Cooper Bridge, near Brighouse, Yorkshire. Again there is a light at the front of the vehicle on either side

26 *Left* The Robinson family in a dog cart with two horses outside the New Hall, Knapton, Norfolk, *c.*1905

27 *Below left* A two-horse carrier's cart at Preston-under-Scar, Yorkshire, about 1911

28 Mr Rotherman's carriage outside the Queen's Head Hotel, Acle, Norfolk. The vehicle is a Double Victoria

31 Nanstallon Forge, near Bodmin, Cornwall, around the turn of the century. A horse is being shoed

29 *Above left* G. Moore, the shoemaker of Witton, near Norwich, with his assistant outside their shop in 1912. The donkey is pulling the parish bier

30 *Below left* The country blacksmith and his forge were a common sight before the Great War. This is Mr Blackwell of Henley-in-Arden, Warwickshire, in about 1900

32 Eli Barlow was the blacksmith of
Medbourne, Leicestershire, around
the turn of the century. He was
sufficiently prosperous to own the
horse and cart

33 *Right* A heavy 'lorry' in Aran,
Inishmaan Island, delivering coal. The
scene could be repeated in most
remote rural areas

35 Farm staff sit on a long cart at Home Farm, near Newcastle-upon-Tyne, about 1900

34 *Left* Filling the village water-cart from the local stream. The view in north Yorkshire could be repeated for many rural villages

36 *Left* A father lifts his small daughter into the horse bus outside the station at Bolton Abbey, Yorkshire, sometime just before the Great War

37 *Below left* The coach survived in the countryside for a very long time after the coming of the railways. This is *The Standard* of Pendeen, Cornwall, in the 1890s, although surprisingly it was pulled by only three horses

38 The Point of Ayr lifeboat in Flintshire being pulled by six horses

39 *The Alert* was the Barnstaple and Woolacombe coach in September 1896. It was well-patronised

40 *Above* An unknown house near Salisbury, *c.*1912, with the coachman ready to drive his master's sporting phaeton

41 *Right* At Burlingham Hall, Norfolk, the carriage horse being used to pull the lawnmower. Both this and a photograph at the same house of the carriage horse being used to drive a potato-cutter by means of a makeshift horse-mill probably date from the 1880s. They show how much the horse at a country house was a working horse.

THE
COUNTRY HOUSE

42 The house and the horse are
unknown; the photographer was
Henry Fox Talbot; the date around
1843. Fox Talbot, pioneer
photographer, worked at Lacock in
Wiltshire, which may be the location

43 Lady Maureen Stewart on her
pony, probably 1907

44 *Right* A Dublin jaunting car

LEISURE and PLEASURE

45 King Edward VII and the King of Portugal, 1909

47 Mr Podmore in his tandem at Knowle, September 1890

46 *Left* Madame de Falbe in her phaeton in the grounds of Luton Hoo in the 1880s. The lady was the wife of the Danish ambassador in London and a very expert horsewoman

48 *Above left* Maids serving refreshments to the Surrey Union Hunt at Old Dene, near Dorking, Surrey, March 1912

49 *Below left* Four horsemen at Evington Fields, Leicestershire, March 1913. They were Captain Harlings, Colonel Peake, Captain Read and Major Plant. The last-named was also known as 'The Count'

50 Major Plant at a meet of Mr Fernie's hounds at Houghton-on-the-Hill, Leicestershire, about 1913

52 *Right* Goodwood Racecourse, about 1910

53 *Below right Persimmon* won the Derby in 2 minutes 42 seconds in 1896 and the St Leger in 3 minutes 20 seconds in the same year. He was owned by the Prince of Wales and was a bay colt whose sire *St Simon* also sired *Diamond Jubilee*, the winner of the Derby in 1900. The latter, also owned by the Prince of Wales (later Kind Edward VII) won both the St Leger and the Two Thousand Guineas. *Persimmon* went on to be the leading sire of 1912 when his progeny won prize money totalling £21,993

51 Mr Belsoe riding *Young Brag* at the Quorn Hunt steeplechases, about 1912

55 *Right* The scene at Epsom, 26 May 1909, when King Edward VII led in his fourth Derby winner. *St Simon* won in 1887, *Persimmon* in 1896, *Diamond Jubilee* in 1900 and *Minoru* in 1909

54 *Pretty Polly* is one of only nine fillies since 1880 to have won the St Leger. This chestnut filly ridden by W. Lane won the Doncaster classic in 1904 in 3 minutes 54 seconds at odds of 2 to 5. Her winning margin of three lengths was the same there as in the Oaks and the One Thousand Guineas which she won for Major Eustace Loader at odds respectively of 8 to 100 and 1 to 4. Her winning time in the Oaks was 2 minutes 45⅕ seconds; there were four starters. Among her descendents is the famous *Brigadier Gerard* who won 17 out of his 18 races, including the Two Thousand Guineas in 1971

56 *Left* A ride along the prom was a popular diversion with the growth of seaside holidays in late Victorian England. The Yarmouth brakes were pulled by a single horse, but two-horse charabancs were used for larger groups. A crowded day by the Yarmouth jetty in the 1890s

57 *Below left* Donkeys on the sands at Cromer with the ladies riding side-saddle in the 1880s

58 *Below* Pottergate, Norwich, in June 1914 when the coal-cart Sunday School treat was about to leave for Ketteringham, where the tea and games which comprised the treat were held in a field lent by a local landowner. Various companies lent vehicles to take the children. The leading cart was owned by Moy's Coals and the covered van by Trevor Page and Company, Cabinet Makers and Upholsterers, Exchange Street, Norwich. Among the Sunday School workers were Ernest Wheeler, of Valentine Street, a chemist at the mineral water depot and Fred Jewing, a cycle dealer, of Chapel Field Road. The secretary was E.J. Cooper, the father of the photographer

59 Sanger's Circus parading through George Street, Luton, in the 1890s. The great strength of horses as a tractive power is aptly illustrated by the eight horses pulling the float. Early motor engines were described in terms of their horsepower

60 A brewer's dray drawn by a
single horse made an ideal platform
for a float in a May Queen procession

62   The fall in the average working week to under 60 hours in the 1890s
and the almost universal adoption of the Saturday half-holiday for industrial
workers, partly due to the popularity of watching association football from
the late 1880s onwards, led to increased leisure in late Victorian and
Edwardian England. Part of this free time was often taken up by a ride on a
horse omnibus to a small public house or country inn a few miles away
from the town. This photograph of the 1890s shows the then newly
instituted service to The Sugar Loaf, Leagrave, from Luton, a distance of
two and a half miles. During the week it was used by villagers wishing to
go into the town. A more traditional conveyance for the latter journey was
the carrier's cart. In the same town, an early trolleybus service had a similar
destination, the hamlet of Round Green, another popular venue for the
Sunday evening excursion for a drink

63 The three-horse bus which went from Brighton Station to the Royal Oak Hotel, Rottingdean, in the 1890s. The journey took an hour

THE TOWN

66 *Above* A single-horse tram of Leicester Corporation Tramways, about 1900. The last horse tram ran on 18 May 1904

64 *Above left* A two-horse bus of Newport Tramways Company, running between the Alexandra Docks and the High Street Station. The photograph dates to before 1886 as the service was withdrawn that year owing to the bankruptcy of the company

65 *Left* An Oxford Tramways Company two-horse bus at Iffley Turn, Oxford, *c*.1910. The driver is Alfred Gardner. The photograph demonstrates how far into the twentieth century the horse bus survived

68 The Guildford fire brigade at the corner of North Street and Woodbridge Road, Guildford, in the period 1865 to 1870. It took four horses to pull the fire engine

69 Funerals for the wealthy, and often the not so wealthy, were often lavish in Edwardian England, with black horses drawing a black-painted hearse with glass sides hung with black drapes. Like the following carriages, the hearse was drawn by two horses. Pall-bearers, men employed by the firm of undertakers, walked beside the cortege as shown in this photograph of a funeral leaving the chapel of rest of Thomas and Edward Neville, undertakers and builders of Castle Street, Luton, in 1907

67 'Robin's Fly' at Melton Mowbray, Leicestershire, was a converted brougham which went to the station to await the trains, in the early 1900s

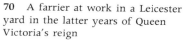

70 A farrier at work in a Leicester yard in the latter years of Queen Victoria's reign

71 A Yarmouth troll cart was a vehicle designed especially to negotiate the narrow Yarmouth rows. The photograph dates to the 1860s and shows one standing on the Hall Quay

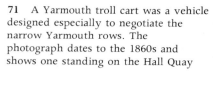

72 The ice froze on the Thames (or Isis) at Oxford in January 1891. On the night before the feat shown in this photograph there had been 23 degrees of frost and the ice was a uniform eight inches thick. James Porter, a livery stable keeper of Christ Church Mews, St Aldate's, Oxford, fitted his horses with shoes held by special wedge-shaped nails to enhance their grip on the ice and drove the carriage for a considerable distance on Monday 19 January 1891. His coach and four weighed nearly seven tons and could do a figure-of-eight turn in the space of a barge's length, yet the ice held

73 The versatility of the horse is shown by this photograph of Magdalen Street, Norwich, at the time of the August 1912 flood when the river Wensum rose 16ft 6½ inches, a foot higher than the previous record of 1614

74 Food, especially meat and groceries, was usually delivered to the door of all except the poorest households in late Victorian and Edwardian England. Most retailers in towns kept one or more delivery carts to do their rounds. William Panter, Family Butchers and Game Dealer, of 34–36 Park Street, Luton, was typical of the more established merchants whose turnover permitted them to run three small box-carts each drawn by a single pony. The meat was kept in a panier behind and beneath the driver's seat. On some models the box could be removed and the cart converted for use by the shopkeeper and his family as a Manchester cart

75 The mayoral carriage was a ceremonial use of the horse in Edwardian England. In the carriage are J.H. Jackson, mayor of Rochester, 1912/13/14, his sister Miss Lucie Jackson, the mayoress, and the town clerk, Apsley Kennett, and his wife. The city mace-bearer sits on the box with the mayoral coachman

76 H.P. Ryland, High Sheriff of Warwickshire, at the Victoria Law Courts, Birmingham, in 1897

77 King Edward VII riding in an open carriage in Dublin. The two footmen have control of the brake, but the carriage is steered by the liveried soldiers sitting on the nearside horses of each of the pairs. There were probably four pairs to such a carriage

78 London Bridge, symbol of a city, and already by 1893 when this photograph was taken, the scene of traffic jams

LONDON

79 The scene is not unique to London, for a street scene filled with horses could be found in any large town and in many smaller ones. This is Oxford Circus in 1893

80 Outer London, too, had a crush of traffic. This is the southern end of Hampstead Road, on 7 April 1904

81 A hansom cab outside the Albert
Hall in 1900

82 The Drive and Rotten Row in Hyde Park, 1893. The Drive was for those who were driven in their carriages; the Row for those who rode. To drive or to ride was a privilege reserved only for the highest ranks of society as horse, groom and carriage had by convention to be immaculately turned out

83 The drive at Hyde Park, 1890s

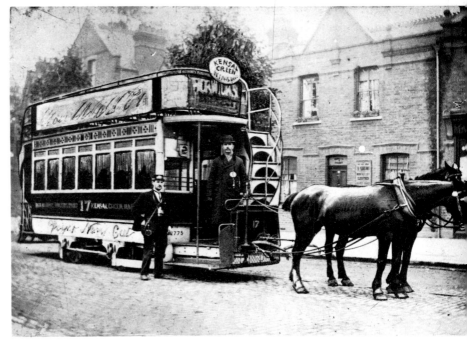

84 A London 'bus; the garden seat 'bus of 1890 outside 'The Queen of England', Goldhawk Road. As with provincial buses, it was covered with advertisements

85 A two-horse tram going to Kensal Green

INDUSTRY

86 *Left* The building trade was circumscribed by the distance a cart and horse could travel in a day and return before nightfall. This Birmingham view of July 1901 shows the horse's summer head-dress as the working horse eats his meal while standing in the shafts

87 *Below* The working horse is here treading a defined circular path on a clay mill in Norfolk in the 1880s, a scene typical of any small brickyard or pottery works in late-Victorian England. The horse turned a rotary puddler which crushed the clay into fine particles

88 A patient wait while the turves are loaded into the high-sided cart at Sidmouth, 1903. Turves were used for fuel and sometimes for roofing

90 Adswood and Bury New Road, Manchester, 29 April 1902. The long train of horses and waggons are setting out for Bury. The scene could be daily repeated in any major town

89 Almost any heavy load required more than a single horse. Three horses in tandem pull the waggon loaded with rolls of paper at Alton, Hampshire, about 1900

91 The last horse-drawn vehicle leaving the Post Office, Penzance; motor vehicles were thereafter used on all the routes

93 House-moving before the advent of the motorised pantechnicon required three horses to pull the van. A.R. Williams of Bargoed ran the 'Gwalia' van in the early 1900s. Long-distance moving was rare but when done was accomplished by means of a sealed van, packed at the house and then lifted on to a flat railway truck for the journey across England

92 The drink trade employed literally thousands of horses. This is a maltster's cart on Hall Quay, Great Yarmouth, c.1885. The single-horse cart was designed to be especially narrow so as to penetrate some of the Yarmouth rows, entrances to which can be seen between the buildings

94 A well-turned-out lorry tandem could command a prize at any show. This is John Power and Sons, of Dublin, whiskey merchants, who won first prize in the 1892 Dublin Horse Show for a lorry tandem

95 A Guinness waggon. It was number 8 of their Dublin fleet

96 A brewer's dray arriving at the Grenadier Guards' barracks, London, 1896

97   Prize-winning horse and cart
outside the Mountjoy Brewery,
Dublin, 1893

99 Loading mustard for the
Admiralty at J. and J. Colman's
Carrow Works, Norwich,
11 November 1897. Three horses were
needed to pull the railway truck. The
original photograph is a Platinotype.
Another Platinotype taken on 5 June
1896 shows a variety of vehicles,
both waggons and carts, at the
Carrow Works; in that picture
eleven horses are visible

98 Non-alcoholic beverages too had an army of horses. Outside Burgess Mineral Water Factory and Plant, Oxford Road, Luton, in 1907

100 The hat trade of Luton used horses and horse-drawn vehicles for a multitude of short journeys. The dray was the commonest vehicle, of which no fewer than 103 operated in the town in 1905, with both the Great Northern Railway and the Midland Railway prominent among the carters, owning more than two-fifths of the total. These two drays of the Midland Railway are collecting finished hats from the warehouses of Richard Burley, of Old Bedford Road, which can be seen in the background. The foreman, standing, was H. Norton; the two drivers were Joe Norris and Richard Oliver. The packed crates were for export; straw hats went as far afield as Australia

102 Even the new technologies of Edwardian England found a place for horses in their factories. Skefco came to Luton, Bedfordshire, in 1911 and built their first factory on Leagrave Road. To transport ball bearings and their component parts round the factory the firm employed at least three horses and drays, two of which can be seen in this photograph of the dispatch bay about 1913

101 A large firm often had its own horse-drawn fire engine, or, as with J. and J. Colman's of Norwich, two engines, each of which required two horses to pull it. The photograph was taken on 26 June 1908

104 Removing the stent or overburden in horse-drawn waggons running on tracks at a china clay pit about 1910

103 China clay, as with many other extractive industries of Edwardian England, used horses in large numbers. Here railway sleepers are being moved to make a track for the first excavator at the pit of the West of England and Great Beam Clay Co. Ltd., in 1908

105 Loading China Clay at
Charlestown Harbour, St Austell

ESTOWN HARBOUR, SHIP A CLAY.

MILITARY HORSES

106 *Left* The Drum Horse of the
17th Duke of Cambridge's Own
Lancers in 1890. The horse was
reputed to be 20 years old at the time

107 *Below* A member of the 5th
Dragoon Guards in the camp in the
Crimea, 1854

108 *Left* An officer and his lady in the Crimea, 1854; it is thought to be Captain and Mrs Duberley

109 *Right* Colonel Lord George Paget of the 4th Light Dragoons on his charger with Lieutenant-Colonel John Douglas of the 11th Prince Albert's Own Hussars, in the Crimea, 1854. The photograph was reproduced and printed on carbon by Jabez Hughes, 1883

110 *Left* Pre-Boer War photograph of Mr White on horseback. It is interesting to observe that the Derbyshire Yeomanry were ordered to place folded blankets under the saddle in place of stuffed pommels

111 *Right* Lord Charles Cavendish Bentinck D.S.O., who joined the 9th Queen's Lancers as a Second Lieutenant on 8 June 1899. He was mentioned in dispatches in the Boer War in June 1900 and promoted to Brevet Major in November of that year. He retired from the regiment in January 1906. The photograph shows him in Full Dress prior to a review by Queen Victoria, *c.*1899

112 Trooper P.W. Samways of the
Derbyshire Yeomanry at Chatsworth
annual camp in 1906. In 1935,
Squadron Quartermaster Sergeant
Samways received the Long Service
and Good Conduct Medal from the
Marquis of Huntingdon

113 Mr Stenson Turner, a trooper in the Leicestershire Yeomanry, *c.*1875–1880

114 The Hampshire Yeomanry in Katharine Street, Croydon, 19 May 1896, awaiting the arrival of the Prince of Wales (later King Edward VII)

115 The Derbyshire Yeomanry on parade at their annual camp in the grounds of Chatsworth House, the Duke of Devonshire's estate. The camp and exercise period lasted about eight days each summer in the 1890s and through to 1914

117 The Drawing Room Parade at Albany Barracks, London, 1893. The eight acres of barracks included one of the largest drill areas in London. The photograph shows a detachment of the Life Guards and the Queen's Trumpeters, with gilded coats and jockey-like caps, on parade prior to attending the social function of a Drawing Room at Buckingham Palace

116 The Trumpeters of the Lincolnshire Imperial Yeomanry, *c.*1903, under Trumpet-Major Collier. Major Collier later served in the Great War; he was photographed in 1916 in field service uniform

118 The farriers of the Second Life Guards shoeing a horse, at Hyde Park barracks in 1890

119 Branding horses purchased for the army at Norwich Cattle Market; thought to have been taken in 1914

120 *Next page* Lord Kitchener in the uniform of Commander-in-Chief, India, 1902–1909